Written by **KORI & SAMMY BARTON**   Painting

B is for Brentwood

An A-Z Journey Through
Brentwood, California

This book is dedicated to all of the past, current, and future farmers and farmhands in Brentwood. We are so thankful for all of the hard-work, expertise, and love that you pour into your produce. Our family has made wonderful memories at your farms and enjoyed the fruit of your labor for four generations, and counting! (Psalm 145: 15-17)

♥ K.B. & S.B.

Foreword

It is with great pleasure that I introduce *B is for Brentwood*, a tribute to the vibrant and storied community of Brentwood, California. This book represents a labor of love, crafted through the shared insights, experiences, and memories of many who know and cherish this truly special place. Through Kori's beautiful illustrations that fill these pages, you'll discover the charm, resilience, and richness that make Brentwood more than just a city—it's a place that embodies the warmth of our friendly community.

Whether you're a lifelong resident, a newcomer, or a visitor passing through, *B is for Brentwood* offers a heartfelt exploration of what makes our city unique, with a sprinkling of insights from some of our beloved community builders. From its agricultural roots and historic landmarks to the local traditions that bring us together, this book serves as both a celebration of our past and an invitation to experience all that Brentwood has to offer. We are so fortunate to have the stories of the past meticulously preserved, and enthusiastically shared by our friends at the East Contra Costa Historical Society (which I would encourage everyone to visit!).

May this collection of Brentwood highlights inspire you to see Brentwood through the eyes of those who call it home and appreciate the legacy that continues to shape its future.

Amy Tilley
Former Executive Director, Downtown Brentwood Coalition
Brentwood Resident and Enthusiast
November 2024

Note From the Authors

It is simply not possible squeeze a city's fullness into a few dozen pages and 26 paintings. The unique places, people, and compelling stories that make Brentwood special are countless! While many treasured destinations, history, and anecdotes could not be included, we hope that the sites and activities highlighted in the following pages kindle your desire to dig deeper into local history and inspire thankfulness for the beautiful place you call home.

The books in our Hometown Highlights Alphabet Series – including *C is for Concord*, *W is for Walnut Creek*, *C is for Clayton*, *B is for Brentwood*, and those still to come – overflow from our hearts of thankfulness for the beautiful communities where God has placed us. What began as a fun project to give to our children grew into a gift of love for our community at large.

There are many wonderful aspects that we *love* about writing and illustrating books, but we are particularly thankful for the connections with locals that we have made (and continue to make) on this journey. We hope that the paintings, poems, and history within these pages makes you smile and encourages you to learn more and go EXPLORE.

♥ *Kori & Sammy Barton*

Visit us online | WWW.HOMETOWNALPHABET.COM

Instagram @HometownHighlightsAlphabet | Facebook Hometown Highlights Alphabet Series

Contents

*A stands for the **AQUATIC COMPLEX**, where taking,*
a swim in the summer can keep you from baking!
Enjoy their three pools
and their fun water features,
and learn how to swim
from their excellent teachers.

A

Since its grand opening in 2000, the Brentwood Family Aquatic Complex has been a popular place for locals to cool off during hot summers. The complex offers three large swimming pools that hold about 577,000 gallons of water combined (nearly the amount of water in an Olympic-sized pool!). The city's Recreation Coordinator, Rachel Owen, loves that the aquatic complex, "offers a variety of opportunities and activities for our community, including providing a great first step into the professional world for our local teenagers who work at the pool each summer." The complex employs about 115 staff annually, including 95 lifeguards that are trained well and work hard to keep everyone safe and happy in the water. With huge water slides, diving boards, water features, classes, and events, this spacious swim center welcomes around 35,000 people each year (and counting).

The letter B stands for the BYER/NAIL place,
a charming old home
that is bursting with grace.
It was built to host travelers
coming by train,
but when the station was built,
that plan went down the drain.

B

Pioneer Johnson Fancher built a two-story home in 1878 (pictured) as a boarding house for travelers. His plan was disbanded, however, when the train station was built five miles away; too far for weary travelers to get to easily! He sold the land to the Byer family in 1883, who then sold it to the Nail family in 1922. When the Nail family donated the land and beautiful home to the East Contra Costa Historical Society in 1984, volunteers eagerly began restoring the home to its original splendor. Since its public opening in 1986, the home-turned-museum has welcomed thousands of visitors of all ages, including school field trips for local students who come to experience what life was like in the 19th and 20th centuries. Museum volunteers continuously maintain the grounds and artifacts so that this beloved parcel of living history will remain highlighted in the Brentwood community for many years to come.

C stands for **CLUSTERS** of grapes on the vine,
they squish them and press them
to make fancy wine.
Some people stomp grapes
into wine with their feet,
you might think that sounds gross,
or you might think it's neat!

C

Much of Brentwood's fertile soil was covered in lush grape vines during the early 20th century. Grapes grow in clusters along vines, and the clusters vary in size, shape, and color depending on the variety. Brentwood's warm climate and cool nights create the ideal environment for growing grapes that made top-notch wines. However, during the 1920s prohibition when selling alcohol was forbidden, many of the farmers who grew grapes for winemaking turned their vineyards into fruit orchards. Vineyards made a comeback in Brentwood in the 1990s beginning with Tom & Becky Bloomfield, whose family has been farming in the area since the 1940s. "We love that we can continue the lineage of Brentwood's agriculture on our family ranch," says Becky. "Grapes are delicious and good for you," whether eaten fresh, dried into raisins, or made into juices and wines.

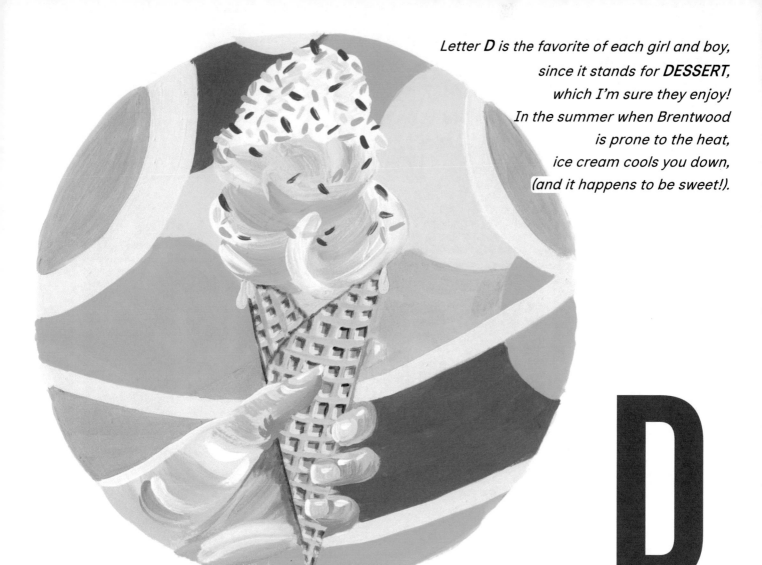

*Letter **D** is the favorite of each girl and boy,*
*since it stands for **DESSERT**,*
which I'm sure they enjoy!
In the summer when Brentwood
is prone to the heat,
ice cream cools you down,
(and it happens to be sweet!).

D

It is not uncommon for temperatures in Brentwood to reach 100 degrees in summer, so locals appreciate creative ways to cool off, especially in the form of dessert. "In Brentwood, where community and connection are at the heart of everything, ice cream has become more than just a treat—it's part of our shared experience," says long-time Brentwood local and Sip and Scoop founder, Vicky Little. Each month, this shop serves about 960 gallons of ice cream in more than 40 different flavors; that's enough to fill more than two backyard hot tubs with ice cream every single month! "Being part of people's memories and milestones—like a child's first ice cream cone or a celebration of good grades—makes this more than just a business," says Vicky, "it's a meaningful way to connect with my community." Do *you* have a favorite ice cream flavor?

Nowadays kids do school from all over on Zoom,
but imagine your whole school
crammed in just one room!
If you'd like to experience
how class used to be,
visit *EDEN PLAIN SCHOOLHOUSE,*
which starts with an *E.*

E

Between the mid-1800s and early 1900s, a simple one-room schoolhouse was typical in rural areas of America and in many other countries. One such schoolhouse was built on Eden Plain Road in 1868 for children living nearby. The Eden Plain Schoolhouse (pictured) was used until 1906 when it was replaced by a larger two-room schoolhouse. A family named Moody used the schoolhouse as their home for a time, and in 2003 it was donated to the East Contra Costa Historical Society and moved to the Byer/Nail House property. Volunteers worked tirelessly to restore the building to its original purpose and acquired desks and furnishings from the early 1900s to transform it into living history. Local elementary school students enjoy visiting this schoolhouse to see what education was like for kids just like them living in the town over 150 years ago!

F stands for **FLORA & FAUNA**, two words,
which in Latin refer to
plants, critters, and birds.
Some sleep through the day,
and we call those nocturnal,
the sleepers at night
just like you, are diurnal.

F

The Brentwood area is home to many wonderful plants and animals of all colors, shapes and sizes. Some of the mammals you might see wandering around local farmlands include coyotes, deer, raccoons, skunks, squirrels, rabbits, and even bobcats. If you look to the sky you might spot a golden eagle soaring overhead, owls silently hunting for their breakfast at twilight, or hummingbirds (pictured) flitting to-and-fro, eating bugs and pollinating plants. And speaking of plants, stately native oak trees provide shade, food, and shelter for many of these local animals. Colorful golden poppies (our state flower), sunflowers, and other wildflowers cheerfully spread their colors as they grow on the side of the road. And you can't help but smile when you see orderly rows of cornfields, and fruit trees nearly bursting with juicy cherries, apricots, peaches, and nectarines. Brentwood is simply teeming with nature at every turn!

Letter G was important for Brentwood to grow, since it's found in the name "Balfour, GUTHRIE & Co." They were experts in farming and unleashed the potential, for the right crops to thrive when the rains weren't torrential.

G

Have you ever been to Balfour-Guthrie Park, or driven on Balfour Road? These were named after Balfour, Guthrie & Co., an expert agriculture and shipping business established in San Francisco in 1869 that shaped the Brentwood community during the early 1900s. They built magnificent buildings (such as the Brentwood Bank, now home of The Press newspaper), introduced new fruits and veggies to local farming, mapped out farmlands, created sewer systems and telephone systems, paved streets, and established a watering process for farmlands that had previously relied on rain alone. This revolutionized farming and Brentwood continued to soar in agriculture production, swapping wheat fields for profitable orchards. They also planted sprawling orchards and owned packing houses (pictured) to prepare produce for shipping around the world. So, the next time you play at the Balfour-Guthrie Park, remember that there is a lot of history in that name.

H is for **HARVEST TIME**
formed to introduce
you to local farms growing
your favorite produce.
If you seek fruits and veggies
of most any kind
their great map makes them simple
and easy to find.

H

A handful of local East Contra Costa County farmers created an organization in the 1970s called Harvest Time that would enable them to connect with the community, market their fresh produce, and educate the public about farming. You may recognize the names of some of the first members including George Nunn, Tino Bacchini, Lee Laird, Gene Stonebarger Sr., Jack Bloomfield, and John Slatten. Harvest Time's membership steadily increased, and they created a trail map highlighting growers, such as Three Nunns Farm (pictured). This map enabled locals and visitors to easily find the farms and enjoy their fabulous produce and other items they had to offer. The original paper trail maps have gotten high-tech upgrades since the '70s, making it easier than ever to plan out a route and connect with over 60 local farms. This non-profit group continues to market local U-pick farms, wineries, and shops to support Brentwood's incredible agriculture for generations to come.

I stands for INSECTS, especially bees,
which pollinate flowers and bushes and trees.
Look close at these creatures
who buzz high and low,
they're fun to examine
and they help our food grow!

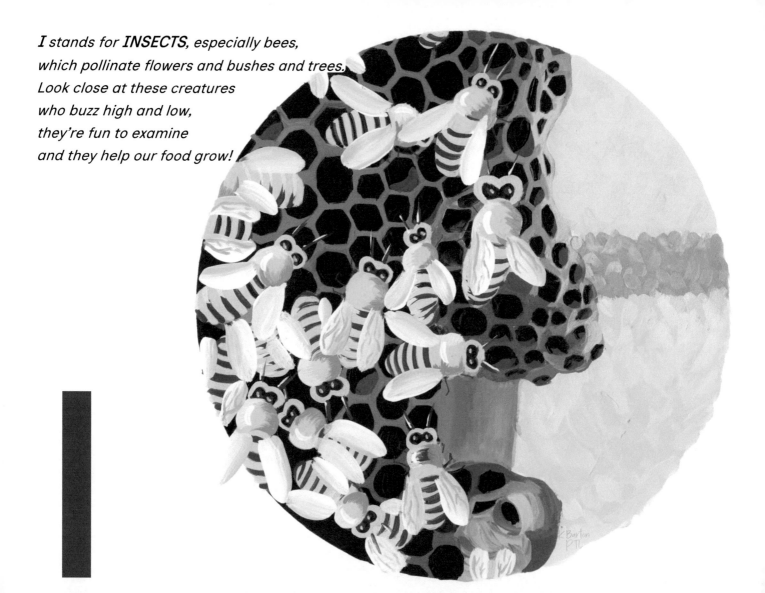

Did you know that Brentwood's flourishing produce is supported in large part by beneficial insects? Beetles, praying mantises, crickets, wasps, bees, and others, all work together to pollinate local fruits and vegetables. Native bees in particular are incredibly helpful for our agriculture. They collect pollen from flowers on the tiny hairs covering their bee body, which scatters on the next flower they land on, and so on. Busy bees may visit up to 5,000 flowers each day! Though they sometimes have a reputation for being frightening because of their stinger, local beekeeper, Kelly Knapp, of Miss Bee Haven Honey, has learned that, "bees are not scary, they are just doing their job! Bees wake up and go to work gathering nectar and pollen and bring it back to their hive." So the next time you see a bee buzzing past, "bee" thankful that they work so hard so that you can enjoy an abundance of local produce!

J is for **JOHN MARSH**
and his house, which still stands,
the first doctor, it's said,
to come to western lands.
His house, though quite splendid,
now needs a restore,
and we hope it gets one
to be admired once more.

J

Early pioneer John Marsh was born to a Massachusetts farming family in 1799. He studied medicine at Harvard, and then a series of difficult life circumstances brought Dr. Marsh to California in 1836. He became the first known Harvard graduate to pioneer to the west, and the first known Western medicine doctor in the West. He purchased about 52,000 acres of land called Rancho Los Meganos from a fellow named Jose Noriega in 1837 for $500 (about $20,500 in today's money) and began a life of ranching and farming. On this land he built a grand three-story stone mansion for his wife. Sadly, his wife Abby died before the home was completed, and Dr. Marsh himself only lived in it for a few weeks before he died. The home was later damaged in earthquakes and it still awaits full restoration. Perhaps someday you will get to see the stone house as splendid as it was in the 1800s.

K stands for **KID-FRIENDLY**,
which describes Brentwood well;
if we list all the ways,
there'd be too much to tell.
When you grow-up, you'll recall
the fun things that you did,
and that Brentwood's a
great place for being a kid!

K

Brentwood is a magical place to be a kid! A host of year-round events and activities encourage family time and celebrate the playfulness of childhood. Summers can be spent swimming at the Family Aquatic Complex, picking fruit at local farms, and visiting family-owned ice cream parlors around town. The fall brings pumpkin picking and corn mazes, and winter hosts a sparkling annual parade and tree lighting event. Spring is a great season to enjoy the local Los Vaqueros Reservoir, play at dozens of playgrounds, and exercise along 80 miles of trail systems. Between the City of Brentwood, the Chamber of Commerce, and The Downtown Brentwood Coalition (among others), local kids can also participate in many special activities and competitions throughout the year, such as cornhole, jenga (pictured), and a classic water balloon toss.

*L is for **LIBRARY**, a place to discover,*
thousands of books,
paperback and hardcover.
The topics are endless,
learn brand new techniques;
take many books home
and return in three weeks.

L

The public library in Brentwood began with a modest library on the campus of Liberty High School around 1908, and in 1914 a library was built at Oak Street and First Street. This library was cherished for a few short years before it burned during a fire in 1919. Salvaged books were moved to a building at Liberty High School. The Brentwood Library Association then purchased that building in the 1920s and moved it to 648 Second Street, where it still stands today. A larger library was built in 1979 that held about 40,000 books, and in 2018 it was replaced by the modern library on Oak Street (pictured). Today, over 16,000 items are borrowed from the Brentwood Library each month. Stop by with your library card to access over 44,000 items in the collection just waiting for you to learn, explore, and enjoy the wonderful world of books!

M is for Farmers' MARKET, so busy!
The hustle and bustle could make your head dizzy.
The produce is endless,
the colors so neat;
you can buy fruits and veggies,
plus flowers and treats!

M

It is only fitting that the agricultural city of Brentwood would have its own year-round Farmers' Market. This market has taken place in downtown every Saturday morning since 2004 and sees around 3,000 attendees each week. Up to 50 local vendors sell everything from just-picked produce, to honey, to fresh cut flowers, and more. Nunn Family Farms has been a part of the market since the beginning and continues to be a crowd pleaser during cherry season. Cheyenne Erickson, Regional Manager for the Pacific Coast Farmers' Market Association, says, "We always love [encouraging] kids to ask questions about the products the farmers are selling. My favorite thing to ask the farmers, if I see a fruit or vegetable I have never tried, is how they like to prepare or eat the fruit or vegetable." Cheyenne loves the welcoming vibe, the, "sense of community, and the diversity of products that the market offers." Visit the market on a Saturday to enjoy farm-to-table produce!

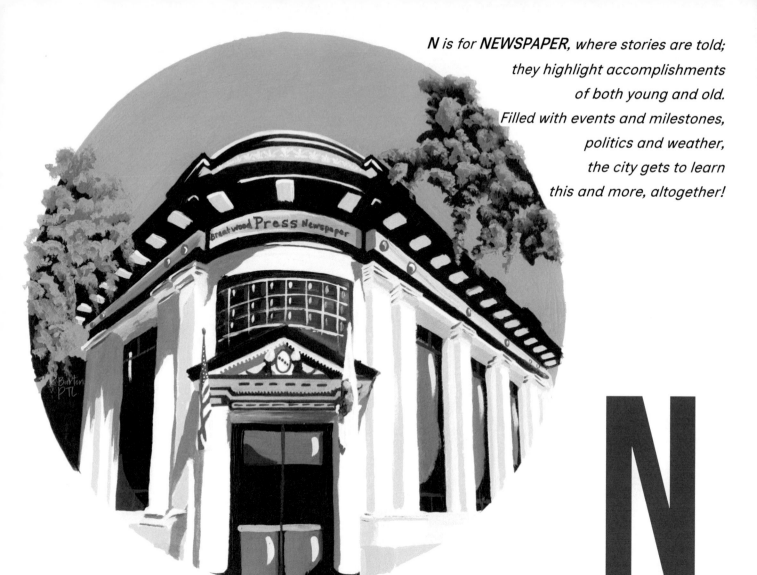

N is for **NEWSPAPER**, where stories are told;
they highlight accomplishments
of both young and old.
Filled with events and milestones,
politics and weather,
the city gets to learn
this and more, altogether!

N

Brentwood's local news has been circulated by newspapers beginning with the Brentwood Courier in 1892, followed by many others over the next century. The Press publishers (building pictured) began in 1999. Greg Robinson was one of the first employees and eventually became the owner in 2013. Greg loves publishing and, "getting to highlight local heroes and their accomplishments." But it is no simple feat! Each issue takes over 200 hours of diligent work from the whole team of editors, production staff, support staff, and more. Greg stresses the priority of good ethics in journalism and that a big part of his job is to keep an eye on things in local government, schools, and to share good news and events in and around the town. "I want kids to understand the importance of journalism," Greg says, "and knowing what's going on in their communities ... printed newspapers may not be around in 10 years, but journalism and local stories will always be around."

O is for OLIVES, whose flavor is seen
by the shade of their color,
black, purple, or green.
They're so tasty and healthy,
we love them to bits,
and a world without olives
would just be the pits!

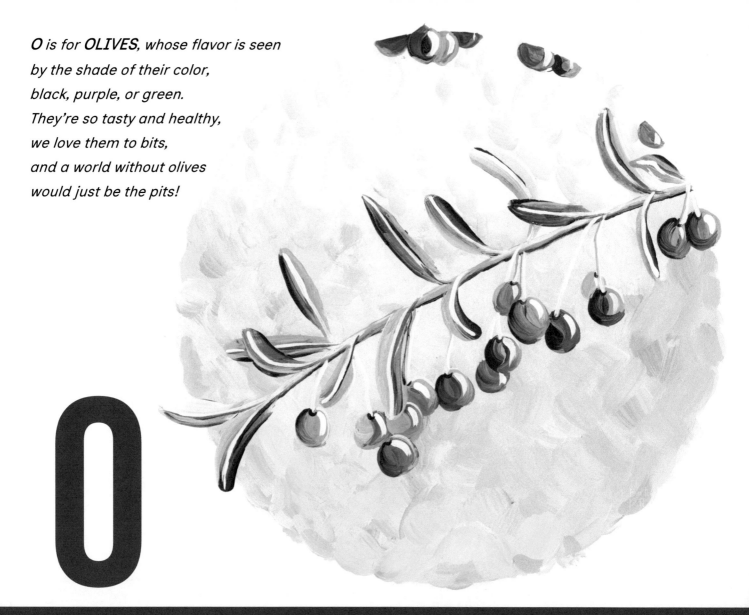

O

With a warm climate well-suited for olive growing, Contra Costa County has been producing olives for pure, top-rate olive oils since the late 1800s. There are many varieties of drought-resistant olive trees, each producing about 20-50 pounds of olives per plant. Sean and Maria McCauley, Brentwood farmers and owners of McCauley Olives, planted 5 acres of olives off of Deer Valley Road in 2000 and now own 300 acres of olive groves among the hills. They love, "the beauty of the orchards, and the satisfaction of growing the olives, picking them, pressing them on our own property, and bottling them in our olive store." Olives are packed with nutrients and belong to the "drupe" fruit family, similar to other stone fruits such as cherries and peaches. The hardy olive trees can live for hundreds of years, producing olives and olive oil for many generations of families!

P is for **PERFORMING ARTS**, on the stage,
with actors and dancers
of most every age.
It's a time to build confidence,
learn brand new skills,
a great performance can give
the audience chills.

P

Many theater organizations have been in the area since at least the 1980s when the Brentwood Community Theatre was established, and others soon followed. "Performing arts plays a crucial role in the fabric of Brentwood," says Nina Koch, founder of East County Performing Arts Center. Nina emphasizes that, "it brings families together and has a profound impact on the lives of young people in our community [through building] confidence [and] fostering creativity." Co-founder of Ghostlight Theater Ensemble, Nancy Torres, notes that, "all of the local schools have stages because performing arts is just so important to our community!" Nina loves, "watching a young performer step onto the stage, sometimes shy at first, and grow into a confident, passionate artist. It is truly magical. The performing arts gives [all ages] a platform to express themselves in ways that are often not possible in other areas of life."

A word to call Brentwood:
QUAINT starts with a Q,
with old-fashioned buildings,
you know that it's true,
that cute structures and history
fill the city jam-packed,
most things are refurbished,
but some remain cracked.

Q

Established in 1870s and later incorporated in 1948, the agricultural city of Brentwood has always embodied the term "quaint." The first building in town was a blacksmith shop built in 1874, which was soon followed by a saloon and a general mercantile store. A massive fire destroyed a number of buildings in 1890, but many of the surviving historic buildings are still in use today as residences, businesses, and offices. The community has worked diligently over the decades to maintain the town's old-fashioned feel, especially downtown (pictured), by restoring treasured buildings such as The Press Newspaper office (the old Brentwood Bank), the Byer/Nail House, and the Veterans Memorial Building. As restoration efforts continue, the quaint feel of the city will abound still more. How many historic buildings can you spot around town?

*The word **RECREATION** begins with an **R**, and to find it you don't have to go very far. Every person in town lives within one-quarter mile, of a trail or park that can make your face smile.*

R

There are wonderful opportunities for outdoor recreation in Brentwood all year-round, and you don't have to go far to find them. Over 80 miles of combined walking trails and bike lanes meander through the city connecting people and places. With more than 100 city parks (including 84 play structures), "every resident is within 1/4 mile of a public park," says Aaron Wanden, Park Maintenance Manager for the City of Brentwood. Some parks in the city include exercise stations, spray parks for kids, all-abilities playgrounds, dog parks, and even a skate park. Aaron and his diligent crew of workers inspect the city's trails weekly and put a tremendous amount of effort into keeping the trails and parks clean, safe, and ready for everyone to enjoy. Aaron's fun challenge to readers is to, "visit every single park ... get out there and head in any direction and at some point you'll run into a park!"

S stands for the grand
SUMMER CONCERTS downtown;
attendees love dancing
and swirling around.
Each week brings a brand
new performer on-stage,
to entertain thousands
of folks any age.

When summertime rolls around, downtown Brentwood is filled with the rollicking sounds of summer concerts each Friday night. Organized by the Parks and Recreation Department, these "Concerts in the Park" have become a well-loved family tradition and welcome about 3,000 people to City Park each week since the summer of 2000. Families bring their blankets, dinners, and lawn chairs to make a full evening of dancing, picnicking, and enjoying the music. The performers vary widely, from jazz ensembles to country bands and everything in between. It is always delightful to watch all of the little kids strutting and spinning along with the music as they create their own original dance moves. This fun-filled weekly event continues to be enjoyed by music lovers of all ages, whether you energetically bounce around or just tap a toe in time with the rhythm.

*The old Delta **THEATER** starts with a T,
it has bright neon lights
on the vintage marquee.
Sit and think as you wait
for your film to commence,
of the old days when tickets
cost just fifteen-cents!*

T

The iconic Delta Theater was built in 1938 with a lofty goal in mind. According to Brentwood local Doreen Forlow, whose parents, Cliff and Rose, were the second owners of the theatre in 1955, the original builder, "wanted to give the local hard-working, prosperous farming community, who had supported his temporary location at the Brentwood Veterans Hall, the best and most modern movie theatre possible." And he did just that. The state-of-the-art theatre changed ownership a few times over 85+ years and was eventually in need of refurbishment. In 2019, Sean McCauley, Brentwood native and owner of McCauley Olives and McCauley Estate Vineyards, began restoration and re-opened in June 2024 with the goal to, "share the experience of Brentwood's history with the community." Sean hopes that kids coming to see a movie will consider the many generations of families who have enjoyed movies in the very same theater through the decades.

There is nothing quite like
fresh fruit warmed by the sun.
When you pick your own fruit
it tastes great and it's fun!
*U stands for **U-PICK**,*
Brentwood's most-loved tradition,
so, go enjoy picking
fruits full of nutrition.

U

Within a 4-mile radius, there are over 50 farms where local families can enjoy harvesting fresh fruits and vegetables straight from the plants. Brentwood isn't named "The U-Pick Capital of the World" for nothing! What began as a single U-pick farm in the 1940s has grown into a popular agritourism destination and a beloved family tradition. Hundreds of thousands of people flock to U-pick farms every year, like the Farmers Daughter Produce farm, owned by Hailey Nunn, a 5th-generation farmer. Hailey loves, "being able to continue my family's wonderful legacy by serving our Brentwood community and providing a fun, educational location for locals and visitors to participate in harvesting ... there is nothing like eating a fresh peach straight off the tree!" From berries to stone fruit, and pumpkins to green beans, there are many varieties of fresh, juicy produce just waiting to be picked by you!

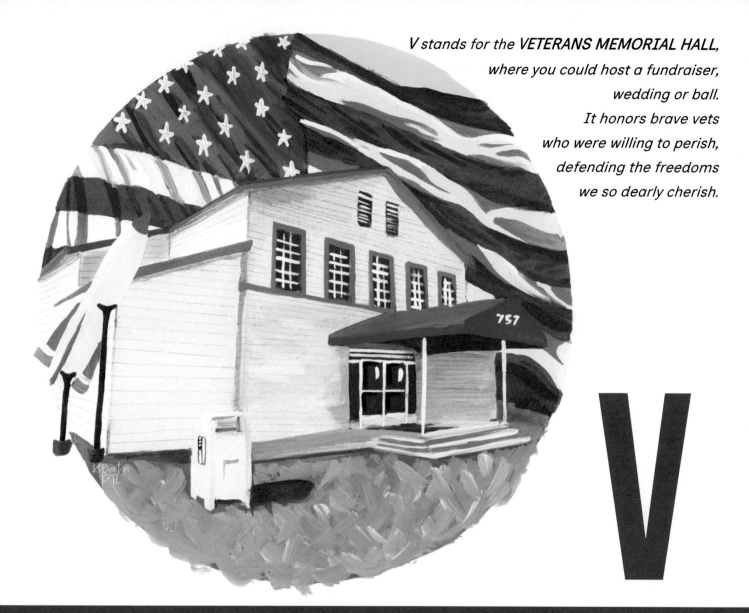

V stands for the **VETERANS MEMORIAL HALL**,
where you could host a fundraiser,
wedding or ball.
It honors brave vets
who were willing to perish,
defending the freedoms
we so dearly cherish.

V

In the early 1900s, the County Board of Supervisors planned to build a veterans memorial hall in each city in Contra Costa County to honor soldiers, sailors, and marines who have served in the United States military. On May 21, 1923, the property deed for a plot of land on 1st Street in Brentwood was approved. The eagerly anticipated grand opening of the Brentwood Veterans Memorial Building was held on September 26, 1925, and was filled with merry dancing and a special celebratory dinner at the stroke of midnight. Since then, this community establishment has held thousands of events including performances, fundraisers, memorials, weddings, birthdays, classes, church services, dances, meetings, and much more. For 100 years, local veterans and other organizations have carefully maintained this building so that it can be enjoyed and preserved for many years to come.

*W is for **WATERSHED**, where rain trickles down,*
it flows from the hills to the Delta past town.
Los Vaqueros' large reservoir
holds water galore,
so we have some to drink
when the rains do not pour.

W

Brentwood is home to the Los Vaqueros Watershed and the Marsh Creek Watershed, where water flows downhill from the hills and Mt. Diablo towards the Delta. Building was completed on the Los Vaqueros Reservoir in 1998 and then the water dam was built higher in 2012 to reach 226 feet high. The reservoir helps to provide flood control, stores fresh water for residents in Contra Costa County, and offers beautiful recreation areas for the community to enjoy hiking, fishing, boating, and picnics. The protected lands also provide a safe place for native plants and wildlife to thrive, such as golden eagles, California tiger salamanders, and San Joaquin kit foxes. The Marsh Creek Reservoir was created in the 1960s by building a dam to control water that flowed from Mt. Diablo to the Delta some 30 miles away. In addition to providing flood control, the creek and reservoir also play an important role for local spawning Chinook salmon on their way to the Delta each year.

*X stands for railroad **X-ING**, where trains, used to rumble through town with fruits, veggies, and grains. They would also take passengers, at least twice per day, carrying folks back and forth from Oakland to L.A.*

X

1878 Became a milestone year for Brentwood when it welcomed its first post office and railroad station on Oak Street (pictured, 1964). Trains along the San Pablo and Tulare Railroad chugged through town carrying travelers, goods, and an abundance of fresh produce from local growers during harvest times. Large blocks of ice were carefully loaded into special refrigerated rail cars called "reefers" that kept fruits and vegetables cool and crisp on their long journeys across the country. In the 1950s, there were at least two Southern Pacific passenger trains that ran daily through Brentwood; the San Joaquin Daylight in the morning and the Owl at night. The last stationmaster to manage this station was kindhearted Mr. Medina, who faithfully stayed at his post until the very last passenger train rolled down the railroad tracks in 1972. Though this train station no longer stands, its memory is kept alive through books, pictures, and heartfelt stories from locals.

*Y is for all **YEARLY FESTIVALS** in town,*
since 1928 they've been the best 'round.
Celebrations for holidays,
and when produce is gathered,
like corn, which tastes best,
when with butter it's slathered.

Y

Various yearly festivals have been celebrated in Brentwood since at least 1928 when the legendary Apricot Festival was one of the most popular events in all of Northern California. This festival was replaced by a Fourth of July fireworks and barbecue shindig called Carnique in the 1950s, and later a Harvest Festival, an Art and Wine Festival, and a corn festival in the 1990s. This CornFest, as it was called, celebrated the prolific local corn crops and was held annually until 2013. Today, there are many jovial festivals in Brentwood that entertain folks of all ages throughout the year. One of the largest modern, annual festivals is the Oktoberfest (pictured), which the Downtown Brentwood Coalition has been organizing since 2007. Recent years have seen over 15,000 attendees at each Oktoberfest. This event, along with others, provide dozens of opportunities for families to enjoy their town and connect with their community.

The Spanish word *MAIZ*, which means corn, has a *Z*,
and in Brentwood there are rows of it
for you to see.
The lush local corn fields
stand proud, due in part,
to the hard-working farmers
that make growing an art.

Z

Brentwood is famous for its prolific sweet corn, called "maiz" in Spanish, which was first planted in Brentwood by Emilio Ghiggeri in the 1940s. His business became G&S Farms (Emilio Ghiggeri & Glenn Stonebarger) and is still family owned over 80 years later. "It's a big joy to keep the family tradition and profession going," says Glenn's son, Michael Stonebarger, "and it is even more rewarding to [develop] a deep connection with the land and community by having a hand in growing food that locals can enjoy in an area that we're all proud to live in." Michael wants readers to know that farming, "is a blend of a lot of hard work, science, land preservation, and dedication that helps put food on our tables and fuels communities." Around 100 people and 15 tractors help during their busy seasons (beginning as early as 3 A.M. each day!) to reap the harvest so that you can enjoy their tasty Brentwood Diamond Sweet Corn!

Location & Contact Information

Brentwood Family Aquatic Complex
195 Griffith Lane
brentwoodca.gov

East CCC Historical Society Museum
Byer/Nail House & Eden Plains Schoolhouse
3890 Sellars Avenue
eastcontracostahistory.org

Bloomfield Vineyards | bloomfieldvineyards.com

Sip and Scoop California
234 Oak Street, Ste B
sipandscoopcalifornia.com

Balfour-Guthrie Park
1701 Balfour Road

Harvest Time & U-Pick | harvestforyou.com

Three Nunns Farms | threenunns.com

Farmers' Daughter Produce
23151 Marsh Creek Road
Farmersdaughterproduce.com

Miss Bee Haven Honey | missbeehoney.com

John Marsh House
Marsh Creek Road & Vineyards Parkway
johnmarshhouse.com

City Events
Brentwoodca.gov
brentwoodchamber.com
brentwooddowntown.com

Brentwood Library
104 Oak Street
ccclib.org/locations/4/

Brentwood Farmers' Market
Oak Street and First Street
pcfma.org/market/brentwood-farmers-market

Old Brentwood Bank
(now The Brentwood Press Building)
248 Oak Street

McCauley Olives | mccauleyolivegroves.com

East County Performing Arts Center
brentwooddance.com

Ghostlight Theater Ensemble | ghostlightte.org

Downtown Brentwood Arch
Oak Street and Diablo Way

Brentwood Parks and Recreation
brentwoodca.gov/government/parks-recreation

The Delta Theater
641 First Street
deltatheater.com

Veterans Memorial Building
757 First Street
bvmb.org

Los Vaqueros Watershed
ccwater.com/726/Los-Vaqueros

G&S Farms | gsfarms.net

Alphabet Check List

CHECK-OFF EACH ACTIVITY AS YOU COMPLETE IT, AND THEN ADD YOUR OWN!

- [ ] Swim at the Aquatic Complex
- [ ] Visit the Byer/Nail House Museum
- [ ] Spot vineyards in the city
- [ ] Try a new ice cream flavor at a local ice creamery
- [ ] Tour the Eden Plain Schoolhouse
- [ ] Look for hummingbirds and wildlife around town
- [ ] Play at the Balfour-Guthrie Park
- [ ] Count tractors in the field during harvest time
- [ ] Look for insects in your backyard or around town
- [ ] Take a peek at the John Marsh House
- [ ] Attend a new kid-friendly event in the city
- [ ] Borrow a local history book from the library
- [ ] Try a brand new fruit or veggie at the Brentwood Farmers' Market
- [ ] Read the Brentwood Press Newspaper
- [ ] Taste local olives or local olive oil

- [ ] Attend a local performance
- [ ] Walk under the arch in downtown Brentwood
- [ ] Take a walk on a Brentwood trail
- [ ] Dance at the summer concerts downtown
- [ ] See a kid-friendly movie at the Delta Theater
- [ ] Harvest produce during U-pick seasons
- [ ] Thank a veteran
- [ ] Picnic at the Los Vaqueros Watershed
- [ ] Spot old railroad tracks in the city
- [ ] Attend one of Brentwood's yearly festivals
- [ ] Taste sweet, local corn on the cob
- [ ] _____
- [ ] _____

Share your adventures with us!
#HometownHighlightsAlphabet
Instagram @HometownHighlightsAlphabet

Bonus Facts

There is some debate whether Brentwood was named after Brentwood in Essex, England, where John Marsh hailed from, or from the short-lived, local Brentwood Coal Company (though most assume the former).

The water tower near Walnut Blvd. is the tallest structure in the city to date. It is now used as a cell tower instead of a water tower, but it has been a local icon for over half a decade.

Only about 5,000 people lived in Brentwood in 1860. Fast-forward 100 years and the population spiked to over 409,000.

Brentwood was incorporated on January 15, 1948 and its boundary covers about 14.8 square miles.

Acknowledgements

Thank you, Cindy Hadden, for your dedication to editing this book and for your support, and excitement along the way. We love you! ♥

We extend our hearty thanks to all members of the East Contra Costa Historical Society and Museum, for your careful preservation of history and eagerness to share their knowledge with us and aid in research, especially Doreen Forlow and Mary Black. In particular, thank you, Doreen, for your time, encouragement, local knowledge, and willingness to answer my questions about Brentwood's rich history!

We made numerous wonderful connections with the community and beyond throughout this project. For permissions, time, knowledge, and support, we are very grateful to each of you who helped shape this book. Thank you!

Downtown Brentwood Coalition (Amy Tilley and Peter Jacoway); Better in Brentwood; City of Brentwood (Rachel Owen and Aaron Wanden); Bloomfield Vineyards (Becky Bloomfield); Our Town Brentwood, CA; Brentwood Library (Natalie Hernandez); The Brentwood Press (Greg Robinson); McCauley Olives (Sean and Maria McCauley); G&S Farms (Michael Stonebarger); The Delta Theater (Sean McCauley); Miss Bee Haven Honey (Kelly Knapp); Pacific Coast Farmers' Market Association (Cheyenne Erickson); Farmers Daughter Produce (Hailey Nunn); Sip and Scoop California (Vicky Little); East County Performing Arts Center (Nina Koch); Friends of the Brentwood Library (William Harms); Ghostlight Theater Ensemble (Nancy Torres); Carol & Clayton Worsdell; Josh Mischel; Bri & Kevin; our parents; and our children ♥

About the Authors

Sammy and Kori Barton are a happy husband-and-wife team, homegrown Bay Area natives, and fellow avid bookworms. They love to use their gifts of language and art to give thanks to God. You'll find them with their kids biking on the trails, hiking in the open spaces, and playing ball at community parks. If you would like to reach out or be notified about upcoming city books in the Hometown Highlights Alphabet Series, please visit:

www.HometownAlphabet.com

References

4th Of July Brentwood News Carnique (July 4, 2024). Courtesy of the ECCHS. Accessed from: https://www.facebook.com/photo.php?fbid=462753583058965&id=100079729822960&set=a.180009664666693

A Little About our Farm (n.d.). Accessed from: https://farmersdaughterproduce.com/about/

About Us: Harvest Time in Brentwood (n.d.). Accessed from: https://www.harvestforyou.com/about-us/

Balfour, Guthrie & Co., Shipping Merchants (1904). Accessed from: https://digitalcollections.lib.washington.edu/digital/collection/advert/id/458/

Bay Area Census, Contra Costa County (n.d.). Accessed from: http://www.bayareacensus.ca.gov/counties/ContraCostaCounty50.htm

Bluelagoon (February 13, 2020). How Many Gallons are in a Hot Tub? Accessed from: https://blspas.com/how-many-gallons-are-in-a-hot-tub/

Brentwood History (n.d.). Accessed from: https://eastcontracostahistory.org/our-communities/brentwood/

Brentwood, CA Oktoberfest (n.d.): Accessed from: http://www.seecalifornia.com/festivals/beer-brentwood.html#google_vignette

Byer Nail Nouse (n.d.). Accessed from: https://eastcontracostahistory.org/museum/byer-nail-house/

California Marsh Creek (n.d.). Accessed from: https://www.americanrivers.org/river/marsh-creek/

CC News (November 9, 2023). Downtown Brentwood Coalition Gets Use Permit for Former Women's Club Building. Accessed from: https://contracosta.news/2023/11/09/downtown-brentwood-coalition-gets-use-permit-for-former-womens-club-building/

Contra Costa County Wine (March 28, 2024). Accessed from: https://www.wine-searcher.com/regions-contra+costa+county?srsltid=AfmBOoqFUkiL13Fmk5SVrnoi5BmeHM57Vn9qwVNmHiom59cOjKDwC_N6

David, Chef (September 22, 2022). Discover Olives: A Stone Fruit with History. Accessed from: https://thejewishvoiceandopinion.com/discover-olives-a-stone-fruit-with-history/

ECCHS Museum Tour (2021). Accessed from: https://www.youtube.com/watch?v=Ghsknmoic5s

Eden Plain Schoolhouse (n.d.). East County Historical Society. Accessed from: https://eastcontracostahistory.org/museum/eden-plain-schoolhouse/

Hartley, Samie (July 8, 2011). CornFest Ready to Rock. Accessed from: https://issuu.com/brentwoodpress/docs/brentwoodpress_07.08.11

Historical Landmarks in Brentwood, CA (n.d.). Accessed from: https://www.amarrealtor.com/area/brentwood-ca/historical-landmarks-in-brentwood-ca/

History of the Hall (n.d.). Accessed from: https://www.bvmb.org/history

Hulaniski, Frederick J., (1917). History of Contra Costa County

John Marsh House (n.d.). Accessed from: https://www.johnmarshhouse.com/

Lafferty, Justin (July 6, 2011). CornFest Grows on Brentwood. Accessed from: https://www.thepress.net/news/cornfest-grows-on-brentwood/article_bc200527-01b0-5cc5-ab10-67e57ddd05f5.html

Lassle, Michelle (n.d.). Harvest Time Brentwood. Accessed from: https://www.betterinbrentwood.com/shop/business-spotlight/311-harvest-time

The History of the Friends of the Brentwood Library (n.d.). Accessed from: https://www.friendsofthebrentwoodlibrary.org/about-friends-of-the-brentwood-library/

Three Nunns Farms (n.d.). Accessed from: https://threenunns.com/about/

References

Leighton, Kathy (March 15, 2021). Footprints in the Sand

Lemyre, Rick (April 27, 2012). Storied Past of Local Fire Service. Accessed from: https://www.thepress.net/news/brentwood/storied-past-of-local-fire-service/article_56cae381-8901-5cf7-832a-0cf44cbe58ad.html

Lemyre, Rick (September 25, 2014). Wanted: The Storied History of the Brentwood Library. Accessed from: https://www.thepress.net/features/wanted-the-storied-history-of-the-brentwood-library/article_0b23c102-44e3-11e4-9fa4-0017a43b2370.html

Levine, Morton (August 29, 2013). Press Ownership Changes Hands. Accessed from: https://www.thepress.net/features/business_profiles/press-ownership-changes-hands/article_7875f334-3c7a-544a-aa08-f31550814d17.html

Los Vaqueros Project History (n.d.). Accessed from: https://www.ccwater.com/435/Los-Vaqueros-Project-History

Marsh Creek Watershed (n.d.). Accessed from: https://www.ccrcd.org/marsh-creek-watershed

Michael, Pamela (2021).State funding moves Brentwood's historic John Marsh House a step closer to restoration. Accesed from: https://pioneerpublishers.com/state-funding-moves-brentwoods-historic-john-marsh-house-a-step-closer-to-restoration/

Mileposts: Bethany, MP 75.7 (June 26, 2024). Railtown Tracy. Accessed from: https://tracyrail.org/mileposts-bethany-ca#more-1798

Miss Bee Haven Honey (n.d.). Accessed from: https://www.missbeehoney.com/

Mydland, Leidluf (Spring 2011). The legacy of one-room schoolhouses: A comparative study of the American Midwest and Norway. Accessed from: https://journals.openedition.org/ejas/9205

Payton, Allen D. (June 12, 2024). Classic on the Outside, Modern on the Inside: Another Sean McCauley success story in East County. Contra Costa Herald. Accessed from: https://contracostaherald.com/historic-refurbished-delta-theater-reopens-in-downtown-brentwood/

San Joaquin Daylight (n.d.). Accessed from: https://tracyrail.org/san-joaquin-daylight-1968

Third Generation Farmers, Quality since the Beginning (n.d.). Accessed from: https://www.gsfarms.net/our-story

Tongson, Sean (April 25, 2024). Brentwood Veterans Memorial Building to celebrate centennial with luau. Accessed from: https://www.thepress.net/features/brentwood-veterans-memorial-building-to-celebrate-centennial-with-luau/article_4abadb66-0324-11ef-8043-2bb576394e56.html

We Eat Well Because Bees Have Hair (n.d.). Accessed from: https://askdruniverse.wsu.edu/2015/02/04/we-eat-well-because-bees-have-hair/ https://harvestforyou.com/pressmedia/the-benefits-of-eating-local-honey/

Made in United States
Cleveland, OH
06 December 2024

11442067R00024

"I'm excited that kids and families can enjoy learning all about the unique history of Brentwood through the ABC's, poetry, and Kori's amazing paintings in *B is for Brentwood*."
GREG ROBINSON I Publisher
The Brentwood Press

"If you're looking for a delightful way to introduce young readers to the joys of fresh food, community, and local culture, *B is for Brentwood* is the perfect choice. This charming children's book takes children on a colorful journey through one our community's beloved farmers markets, where they can meet friendly farmers, discover vibrant produce, and learn about the importance of supporting local businesses."
CHEYENNE ERICKSON I Regional Manager
Pacific Coast Farmers' Market Association

"*B is for Brentwood* is a charming book, beautifully illustrated, that children and parents alike will enjoy as they learn more about the many things that make Brentwood a wonderful place to live."
WILLIAM HARMS I Board of Directors
Friends of the Brentwood Library

"*B is for Brentwood* captures not only the pride locals feel in their family-friendly community, but also provides a wealth of historical information. For each letter, the colorful illustration and simple rhyme engage the reader, and the interesting historical information blends the past with the present, sharing what has made Brentwood a charming place in which to live."
MARY BLACK I President
East Contra Costa Historical Society

"A book that showcases some of the many wonderful things that Brentwood has to offer. A must read for all families!"
PETER JACOWAY I President
Downtown Brentwood Coalition

"[Brentwood] is a neat country village
with broad, smooth streets…"

-F. J. Hulanski

Local historian, 1917